T0267475

advance .
women surrounded by water

"*Women Surrounded by Water* is a memoir-song-ode-manifesto-rosary to the Puerto Rican women of a family with ghosts for men. In the colonial context of the archipelago's countryside, the men look to the national culture for identity and come away broken, while the women look to tradition, love, and religion to escape the guilt of leaving men who must be left. It is a story of betrayals, of oneself and others, and of the hungers of the heart such struggles leave behind. Coral has contained my very history, my heartbreak, along with her own."

—Anjanette Delgado, author of *The Clairvoyant of Calle Ocho*

"Every time I read this memoir, it breaks my heart, yet by the time I finish, my heart feels whole again. These lives and losses leap off the page. Patricia Coral's language is alternately lyrical and lush, bold and unsparing, always with an awareness of history's whetted edge. A stunning debut."

—Sandra Beasley, author of *Don't Kill the Birthday Girl: Tales from an Allergic Life*

"*Women Surrounded by Water* centers on the silenced history of Puerto Rican women and what writer Anjannette Delgado calls 'our sexile.' Colonization, patriarchy, and family tie women to the land differently than they tie men to it. Revisiting the history of her ancestras, Patricia Coral tells her own story while also giving voice to the experiences of three generations of women. Using memory and form to decolonize her storytelling, she invites us to 'senti-pensar' with her the process of becoming a woman writer, a Latina whose voice can shape the fragmented view we have of Puerto Rico."

—Mayra Santos-Febres, acclaimed Puerto Rican author and critic

"Patricia Coral has composed a work so intimate, so faithful a translation of emotion and experience, that it is difficult to call this collection a memoir when it is also poetry and family album and historical testament. But it is memoir in the most urgent sense: with unmatched concision, honest remembrance, and care, the author leads her readers through the heretofore terrifying, now vivifying, waters of life."

—David Keplinger, author of *Ice* and *Another City*

women surrounded by water

machete

Joy Castro and Rachel Cochran, Series Editors

women surrounded by water

a memoir

patricia coral

mad creek books, an imprint of
the ohio state university press
columbus

Library of Congress Cataloging-in-Publication Data
Names: Coral, Patricia (Writer), author.
Title: Women surrounded by water : a memoir / Patricia Coral.
Description: Columbus : Mad Creek Books, an imprint of The Ohio State
    University Press, 2024. | Series: Machete | Summary: "One Puerto Rican
    woman's hybrid memoir in moments, stories, and fragments, exploring
    personal and natural disasters, borderlands, home, self, family, diaspora,
    dislocation, Hurricane Maria, and feminism"—Provided by publisher.
Identifiers: LCCN 2024022862 | ISBN 9780814259252 (paperback) | ISBN
    9780814283738 (ebook)
Subjects: LCSH: Coral, Patricia (Writer) | Women authors, Puerto Rican—21st
    century—Biography. | Puerto Rican women—Biography. | LCGFT: Creative
    nonfiction. | Autobiographies.
Classification: LCC PS3603.O7314 Z46 2024 | DDC 818/.603 [B]—dc23/
    eng/20240724
LC record available at https://lccn.loc.gov/2024022862

Cover design by Nathan Putens
Text design by Juliet Williams
Type set in Adobe Sabon LT Pro

For the women who made me

contents

aislamientos: shore
uno: exiles

dos: storms

tres: burials

camino a casa: ocean

trigger warning

Should I say "trigger warning"? Should I type now Trigger Warning? Do I know what your trigger is? My triggers were hearing sounds of doors opening, a locked restroom door, a shower taking too long. My triggers are phone calls from the island in the middle of the night. How do we name triggers? Should I stop writing about doors, locks, and showers? Trigger warning alcohol. Trigger warning drugs. Trigger warning blood. Trigger warning. Trigger warning. Trigger warning. You might find here triggers.

proyectos domésticos
LAND

the women who
test the waters

Patricia

I was raised to fear the water.

And I grew up in a Caribbean island. It was like being raised to be afraid of myself. They didn't teach me about my strengths, only the dangers of who I was.

I was raised to believe that water could kill me. That I could drown any minute. The beach was dangerous, and I should stay safe on the shore.

I was born in a body they named woman to a family that prefers men.

I was born a redhead in a country of brunettes. Strong-willed for a woman, too talkative for a student, too thick, too masculine to be feminine, too feminine to be masculine.

I was born too everything. An excess. Always out of place. And I was not a man. I was supposed to obey.

I grew up between unwanted stares and invisibility. Excessive control and disproportions.

And sometimes there was also love. When I didn't feel I had to try to apologize for being who I was.

The One Who Learns to Swim in Pools

Abuela built a pool in her backyard for me to swim in, or so they told me, that it was for me. She never learned how to swim, but she wanted me to have a pool. Mami didn't want me to drown, so she took me to swimming lessons, since she couldn't stop her mother-in-law from building a pool. During the first lessons, my mom had to sit on the edge of the pool, her legs inside the water. I'd hold on to them while I learned how to move mine up and down, one leg at a time.

Titi Carla

When I was a child, Titi Carla was my freedom. We had a lot of fun singing loud to Ednita Nazario's songs anytime she drove me around in her red Pontiac. Sometimes she took me to Toys "R" Us and bought me any Barbie or Polly Pockets or Cabbage Patch Kids I wanted. The best days ended with us seated at the edge of the pool, eating a pile of chicken tenders from Golden Skillet, moving our legs inside the water.

As a woman, I could aspire to only two things: to be married to someone, an educated man, or to end up alone like Titi Carla. *Es que ustedes son idénticas.* You are just like her, they used to tell me whenever we were together or I was too angry, or too fat, or too unruly.

My family could see only her singleness, her tallness, her fatness. *Tan sola. Poor Carla. She's bad-tempered because she never got married.* If you didn't have a man who loved you, who could prove you were loveable, you were incomplete. Unhappy. Worthy of pity. A half-human. Women were raised to believe it until they internalized it. Maybe that's why I wasn't afraid to jump into a dysfunctional relationship as soon as I had the chance of love at seventeen.

The Good Girl

I never eloped with the boyfriend they forbade me to be with. I thought I would starve if I did and have to go back defeated to my parents' house. Marriage was expected from well-behaved girls. If they had a little self-respect. God forbid we dared to announce we were going to move in with someone.

I turned twenty-five and married him.

marriage addictions I

I remember how you cried when I walked towards you and took your hand in my hand.

After the wedding, we danced all night in Casa de España to our favorite songs, to our friends' joy, to our love. My feet were aching. When I complained about the pain, you took me to the side of the dance floor and brought a chair for me to sit on. You knelt in front of me, took off my heels, and gave me a foot massage. A friend took a picture of me in my wedding gown with my bare foot in your hand.

I don't have a picture of your forehead cut open, nor of the red blood running through your nose until it reached for your mouth, like a river flowing into the sea.

Our naked bodies on a hotel bed. Your left hand on my breast, your wet kisses on my neck. "My wife, I'm so lucky that you are my wife," you whispered, and I stared at your wedding band shining on your finger.

We were hungry. Late at night we walked hand in hand to Walgreens to get snacks. You chose a box of cheese sandwich crackers, and we went back to the hotel. We sat next to each other at the bedroom balcony and opened up a bottle of rum. Our laughter merged with the sound of the waves and the palm trees in San Juan. We stayed awake till dawn. Until there were no crackers or rum left.

On our first trip together, you let me have the window seat in the airplane. You knew how much I loved it. I fell asleep on your chest while we were up in the air. We opened the tray to fill out the tourist card, took pictures of our left hands with our new wedding rings and the first document we checked "married" on. You carried my luggage when we landed in Punta Cana.

A room with an ocean view. Carefully chosen lingerie. Days spent between the bed and the water. You wrote our names on the sand with a heart and a "Just Married" next to them. You didn't stop taking pictures of me. You didn't stop saying how much you loved me.

I asked you to stop ordering so many drinks at the bar.

✳

It was a Monday. You brought another six pack of Medalla to our house. I threw it to the floor of the unfinished terrace in the backyard and yelled: "I will not allow any more alcohol in this house. I'm tired of it." I was actually tired of you. Maybe I threw the beers to the floor because I couldn't throw you, or my job, or grad school, or our house, or our marriage, or myself. You cried. Right there or later in our bed until you fell asleep. Or so I remember it. Or so I want to remember it, that I paid with guilt for my cruelty.

Some Friday nights made me feel that we were like any other young married couple. You picked up a medium pizza with onions, half bacon, half ham. We sat on the couch to watch comedy movies on the TV your dad bought for us. The dogs lay on the floor right next to us. My dreams were small.

I called my best friend crying.

"We still don't have a dining table at the house," I told her.

"Don't cry! You have a husband that really loves you, and that's what matters the most," she answered. "It takes time to put a house together."

I didn't tell her that you were drinking beers every day and the fridge was almost empty.

I hated being a full-time teacher, a full-time grad student, and a full-time wife. I fell asleep on the couch as soon as I arrived from work every afternoon until the next day. "I feel so alone," you kept telling me over and over, and I didn't listen.

Every few months you cut plantains and green bananas from our backyard, put them inside shopping bags, and gifted them to our neighbors.

When we invited friends over, it took me too long to clean. "Why are you so slow? Stop being so obsessed about the details. Go take a shower, and I'll finish the rest," you told me as you took the mop from my hands. I felt inadequate.

I called in sick to work because our car didn't have enough gas.

You stayed awake all night when I had to finish my final paper. You made me coffee and rubbed my neck. "You've got this. You're almost done. I'm here with you." A few months later you celebrated my diploma by taking a picture of it and posting it on social media with a caption that read, *I am so proud of my wife*.

It was summer and you were wearing a long sleeve T-shirt to cover your arms.

You started losing students. I wanted to think it was because of the economy and not because you didn't make it to the music lessons. You didn't leave the bedroom for a week. When you did, you didn't have a job anymore.

In the mornings I got dressed for work and sat on the bed staring at the floor. It took me an hour to stand up and leave the house while you slept. I was afraid to leave the house for fear

I'd find your dead body lying on the kitchen floor when I came back and opened the door.

You promised to trim the tree that was in front of the house. When I came home from school, I found you crying in the kitchen.

"Are you okay?"

"I killed the tree," you told me. "I cut it too much."

I looked through the window and saw that the tree was missing most of its branches. "Don't worry, it will grow back," I reassured you.

And it did.

a prayer for mercy

Inhale:

Lord, I am miserable.

Exhale:

Like the women of my life were miserable.

don't leave him alone

No lo dejes solo, your mother, grandmother, aunts tell you. *No lo dejes solo,* as if he's going to break, get lost, as if he depended on your breasts to be fed. *No lo dejes solo,* as if he were an elderly man, an infant. *Me voy porque está solo, I can't go because no lo quiero dejar solo. I have to leave, the husband came home early y está solo.* As if the husband could not survive by himself. *No lo dejes solo, nena, no lo dejes solo, trust me.* As if their husbands ever thought, *I am going home because she is alone, because the children are waiting for me, because I have a family,* instead of being at the bar, or in the bed of a stranger. Judge them until you marry. Stop leaving, stop traveling, doing. Hear the chorus of their voices in your head. Get into your cage. Lock the door. *No lo dejes solo, no lo dejes solo, no lo dejes solo.* Rot.

marriage addictions II

We argued on our way to celebrate our anniversary and my birthday. You spent the money we were going to use for the weekend escapade. When we arrived at the hotel you gave me a gift and a handwritten card. The line on the card read, "I'm sorry for not being able to give you all you deserve." And I sobbed.

"These marks are old. Do you believe me?" you asked me while you took off your shirt to get inside the pool and I stared at the fresh red dots on your arm.

"I know," I lied.

I waited for you at my parents' house for a family dinner. "I feel I'm getting sick. I prefer to stay home," you told me when I called you to ask why you were taking so long. When I made it to our house you were dressed up to go out.

"Where are you going?" I asked, and the argument started.

"I'm getting some beers," you answered.

"I'm sick of your drinking. If you are going to keep drinking like that you better not come home," I yelled.

Hours passed by and you didn't return. I was frightened. I thought you were dead. You came back to the house in the morning and told me that you had a relapse. That was the beginning of a war that I will always feel responsible for.

You invited me to a twelve-steps group in Levittown. I went to the family meetings while you went to the recovering addicts meeting. I saw a young woman talking to you outside of the room. She was celebrating eight months of being clean. I remember the fear in her eyes when you told her you were having a relapse after years of being sober. That night you stopped attending the recovery meetings.

An old man from my group lost his wife to drugs. He gifted me a book with a note in the back that read: "Choose yourself."

I took off my wedding rings and put them on the coffee table just before falling asleep on the couch. When I woke up in the morning, I couldn't find them. "Maybe the dog swallowed them by accident," you told me. I wanted to believe you.

You came trembling to the bedroom with a glass of water. You got in the bed, and when you hugged me, your skin boiled hot.

El Dragón song played on your radio. That was your hell anthem. You turned off the bedroom lights and lay in bed for hours staring at the ceiling. The demons were visiting again.

A list of lost items:
1. the gold and diamond watch Abuela gave me

2. the white and blue sapphire necklace that used to be
   Titi Carla's
3. your wedding band
4. did you take mine?

Track marks. Underneath your long-sleeved shirt. Red dots that marked the trail of your veins.

Another list:
 1. your guitar
 2. your drum set
 3. our radio
 4. your bike
 5. your job
 6. my car
 7. hope

I found syringes in the toilet tank. Inside your shoes. I found a spoon in the washer when I was doing laundry. It was bent, burned at the bottom with an uneven black circle.

Our neighbor punched you in the face when he learned you stole his skateboard. Our goddaughter was visiting us. She sobbed when your body hit the floor. I pressed her against my chest.

I was trapped in a never-ending scavenger hunt.

a prayer for miracles

Inhale:

God protect my husband.

Exhale:

Even if you don't protect my marriage.

bisabuela minia

I wonder if this picture was taken before or after your husband hit you. Before or after my grandpa ran away from your house because he couldn't see you bruised, again. Because he knew that at seventeen, he was old enough to defend you next time his dad battered you. You stayed behind with eleven children and black eyes. Was your long-sleeved dress hiding wounds? Did breathing hurt? I wonder if your husband grew tired of bruising your body in your old age. I don't know if this picture was taken before or after my grandpa named my mother Herminia, like you. Before or after she named me Patricia. Your blood is alive in us. We have never been hit by men. But we've been bruised.

the women in the kitchen

In Naranjito, a small rural town in Puerto Rico, there was a restaurant on a mountaintop called El Mesón. It had two lives. In its first life it was a bar, a restaurant that sold lechón and typical Puerto Rican staples, and a tropical dancing place for the locals. After my father bought it, El Mesón was remodeled, transformed into a two-story fine-dining restaurant with a fancy cocktail lounge. It had big balconies around it, and on the second floor, glass to ceiling windows. You could sit anywhere and watch the island like a god on top of a grassy green cloud. In its second life it was ours.

Dad was the only doctor in Naranjito. Whenever we arrived at the plaza in the center of the town, he would keep his left hand outside of the window, to wave at everyone who waved at him.

My father worked at his small medical practice during the daytime. After work, he stopped by the restaurant before coming home, and on weekends we joined him. We barely spent time with him.

On the weekends, we drove on a narrow two-way street to El Mesón. We left behind the safety of the straight, wide roads, the lights of our cities—San Juan, Bayamón, Guaynabo—and drove up twisty rural roads. In the sky there were tall trees, plantain palms, high grass. Fresh air on our faces when our car windows were open. We drove and drove and sometimes I got dizzy with all the twists and turns. After a while, we arrived at a tight winding road called Las siete curvas. We turned left-right-left-right-left-right-left on our way to El Mesón. Once we passed Las siete curvas, it took about twenty more minutes of curves and climbs before we made it to our restaurant.

Mami made us repeat a prayer after her every time we got into the car to go to Naranjito: "Dios Todopoderoso ayúdanos a llegar sanos salvos y tranquilos. Que no le hagamos daño a nadie y que nadie nos haga daño a nosotros."

During daytime the two-story restaurant had a spectacular view of green mountains, colorful rural houses, the main cities in Puerto Rico's north coast, and the Atlantic Ocean. At night, before leaving, the tiny lights from the houses, buildings, streetlamps of Bayamón, San Juan, Guaynabo looked like a lit-up Christmas tree under a starry sky.

At the restaurant I could eat all the food I wanted. It was like having the menu and the kitchen to myself. Shrimps in creole sauce, chicken breast al pimentón, turkey breast in pineapple glaze, mofongo, tostones, and on the best days, grilled lobster in melted butter. Then flan de coco o de queso or tres leches for dessert.

I had a crush on the restaurant's chef. Or maybe I liked that she was a woman in charge of men. Auri was the one giving orders, supervising, leading. She was strong, and the cooks did everything she said. Unlike the women in my life who spent their lives following husbands. I wanted to be like Auri.

We were driving back to our home in Bayamón one day when my dad told my mom that Auri was pregnant with the security guard's child. Rivera was married to another woman. My brother studied with his eldest son, Pedro. We learned that Pedro would have a baby brother, but we were not allowed tell him.

Carlitos was my dad's business partner. One day, Carlitos' wife was pulling her car out of their garage to go to El Mesón, and an elderly woman was walking on the sidewalk. She didn't see her. Carlito's wife just felt something hit her car. He left the restaurant as soon as he got the call.

Carlitos' wife couldn't sleep. She didn't want to live. And she tried and tried and tried not to. Carlitos stayed with her all the time until she was admitted to a mental hospital. He never went to the restaurant again. Not even after she recovered. He said he couldn't help anymore with the expenses. My dad was left alone with the burden.

The locals in Naranjito couldn't afford to go to El Mesón, and the people from the cities were not driving there.

Some weekdays, my dad came home with fresh eggs in cardboard boxes. Other times he arrived with bags filled with roots: ñames, yautías, batatas, yucas. . . . Most of his patients didn't have health insurance, and when they couldn't pay, my dad still treated them, and they gave him gifts.

Auri stopped working at the restaurant. Rivera was not leaving his wife, and maybe she didn't want to be his coworker.

We had more debts than customers, and my dad couldn't come up with the money to pay his employees. The cooks resigned. We had a restaurant without cooks. Tables without customers. At least we had menus, plates, tablecloths, and a view.

Mami, Abuela, and Titi Carla took Auri's place in the kitchen, and sometimes I joined them. There were mountains of white plates, grills with flames that could almost go up to the ceiling, rows of half-served dishes waiting to be served, piles of pots waiting to be washed. It smelled like garlic, burnt meat, wine, butter. There was a beauty to the clanging, the sizzling, to the way the women moved like fire ants escaping a destroyed mound.

My brother knew how to write, so he went to the tables

and took people's orders. His letters were so big, he used one notepad sheet per order instead of having all the table's orders on the same sheet. Customers laughed and were entertained by having a seven-year-old redheaded Puerto Rican boy with blue eyes and charisma taking their orders. They thought it was cute he wanted to work. I wondered if he felt he had no option.

I couldn't find my place in the restaurant. I just walked and observed like a wanderer, a nomad, a homeless ghost. I wanted to stay downstairs in the cocktail lounge where my dad was. He sat at the center of the bar surrounded by friends and visitors. They all sang boleros, décimas, trovas with Laura Rita, our weekend musician. When my dad was not singing, he was making jokes and drinking his whiskey on the rocks. Downstairs it was forever joy, and from time to time I sneaked into the room.

"You can't be here, this is for adults not for girls," my dad would say when he saw me. "Go upstairs with your mom."

Sometimes I joined the women in the kitchen. I cut lettuce and tomatoes to garnish the plates. Or I submerged the pile of dirty dishes in hot water and Clorox and let them take a nap in the sink.

My dad was playing the guitar and smoking a cigar on one of the balconies. He called me over to teach me how to sing.

"Qué maraviiiillaaaa Goooyo, qué maravilla, sing like this."

"Qué maraviiiillaaaa Goooyo, qué maravilla," I sang after him.

"Not like that you're out of tune," my dad said. "again."

I sang and sang until he told me I was doing well. It was a song about the joy of becoming a father.

I sneaked into the cocktail lounge and saw a woman whispering to my dad in his ear. I didn't know if I should tell my mom or keep a secret.

Peel the green plantains, cut them in pieces, fry them, take them out of the oil, and put them in a big wood pilón, add garlic, olive oil, smash it, smash it with the huge pestle, add bacon or chicharrón, drizzle more oil, smash it, smash it, flip the pilón on a plate, and serve the mofongo with chicken, pork, or shrimps.

I was a mouse, eating and hiding in the restaurant.

Musicians, trovadores, whiskey on the rocks. *Papi please let's go we're tired. Not yet. Not yet.* The songs kept going and going. *Si nos dejan, Solamente una vez. Usted es la culpable. El reloj.* My dad had a never-ending nostalgia.

Our days were a perpetual drive through Las siete curvas. Sit in the middle, look to the front so you don't get dizzy. Sit down, put on your seat belt, be quiet. Don't look to the sides. Wait for time to pass and maybe you won't throw up.

I was getting fatter. Eating was an anchor. My mom was getting skinnier.

Dios todopoderoso ayúdanos a llegar sanos salvos y tranquilos. Que no le hagamos daño a nadie y que nadie nos haga daño a nosotros. Dios todopoderoso ayúdanos a llegar sanos salvos y tranquilos. Que no le hagamos daño a nadie y que nadie nos haga daño a nosotros. Dios todopoderoso ayúdanos a llegar sanos salvos y tranquilos. Que no le hagamos daño a nadie y que nadie nos haga daño a nosotros.

My dad in the cocktail lounge. Us, on the second floor.

There was a Christmas party at the restaurant, and my dad was dancing vallenato with Laura Rita's daughter. He was telling her something, and she was laughing. We were sitting in a corner, and my brother was sleeping on my mom's lap.

"I don't want dad to dance with her," I said.

"Go tell him," she answered. As if she were waiting for someone to defend her cause.

Santa María Madre de Dios, ruega por nosotros los pecadores ahora y en la hora de nuestra muerte. Amén.

I started hating going to Naranjito and El Mesón. I was tired of sharing my dad and being invisible.

Count the white lines on the road. Count the cars that are missing a headlight.

"Let's go home, we're tired," I begged my dad.
"Not yet, nena, ya mismo."

I was angry at men. Or maybe at my dad. Or maybe at myself for being born a girl.

"Mami, I want to go home," I said almost crying.
"Tell your dad."
But dad didn't listen to me. Didn't listen to me. Didn't listen to me. *Not yet, todavía, nena. Ya mismo, todavía. Not yet.*

"I'm sick and tired of your behavior," my mom exploded in front of everyone as soon as my dad entered the kitchen. "We're breaking our backs here, and you're singing and drinking in the cocktail lounge."
"I'm working too," my dad yelled. "I'm just entertaining people so they stay longer and order more. They stay because of me." He turned around and slammed the kitchen door. My mom burnt the tostones she was frying. We all kept cutting vegetables, searing meats, washing dishes, sweating in silence.

I felt nauseous, dizzy, as if I had a thousand bees buzzing inside my stomach. Las siete curvas. I wanted to sit in the front with my mom. To become a buffer between her and my dad. *Dios te salve María, llena eres de gracia.* To watch the road as we drove right-left-right-left-right-left-right. Until we made it safely home. My dad was always the driver, even when he had been drinking. *Santa María Madre de Dios ruega por nosotros los pecadores.* He told my mom that I was not nauseous, that I was faking it. And they told me to stay in the back middle seat so I could feel the a/c blowing on my face, to look to the front so I didn't get dizzy. And they drove me and took me wherever I didn't want to go and my mom copilot, copilot, copilot. And I wondered what was wrong, even if I was not sick, that I wanted to sit in the front, next to her.

We lost one of the cars, my dad couldn't pay for it. He started going to his office and the restaurant in public transportation, so my mom could take us to school and run errands.

We stopped going to El Mesón. There were only a few customers, and we were not needed. We spent most weekends waiting for my dad who never came home on time.

My dad carried cologne in his briefcase. Before leaving the house, he spritzed it on himself five times. Once on the right side of the neck, another on the left side, then on his shirt close to his chest area. Right, left, then in the center closer to his belly. He spritzed some more on the palm of his hands and patted his cheeks. He left the house impregnated with sandalwood and us, behind.

One night, my dad asked me to come downstairs to the living room. He was sitting on our couch, staring at the floor, his eyes were red. I sat next to him. He told me that he'd made some mistakes. That he had been seeing another woman and my mom asked him to leave. That he was moving to Abuela's house in the morning. Later, I imagined that the news smashed us in the kitchen of El Mesón late at night and that my mom grabbed our stuff, us, as quickly as she could and went out to the car. Her eyes became a waterfall and her cheeks rocks. She drove fast fast fast until the winding roads felt as straight as a San Juan highway. And I was scared *Dios todopoderoso ayúdanos a llegar sanos salvos y tranquilos. Dios todopoderoso ayúdanos a llegar sanos salvos y tranquilos.* And I was sitting in the front, looking straight through the glass at the lights of the cars, my heartbeat punching the buzzing bees in my stomach. And I held fast to the door handle and didn't look to the sides.

My mom dropped me at school for the last day of fourth grade, and I felt I was going to throw up. I hid in the restroom. I wanted to be with my mom, and my stomach burnt, burnt, burnt until a boiling pebbled river came up my chest and out through my mouth soiling the toilet, the walls, and my uniform.

My mom cried when she thought I wasn't watching. She was disappearing into a skinny body because of her lack of appetite, and I was afraid of losing her. I sneaked into her room at night and slept on the floor while she slept. I left early in the morning so she didn't notice. Whenever my dad came to pick my brother and me up for the weekend, she put on a sexy dress or skinny jeans with a fancy top, put on makeup, high heels, and didn't speak to him. That performance lasted a year.

My brother and I spent the summer in bank lobbies. My mom

always had to negotiate for anything our family needed. Loans, payment plans, extensions. But she always tried to compensate by taking us to a nearby park and buying us piraguas—shaved iced in a paper cone with raspberry, lemon, tamarind, or coconut syrup. As we ate the piraguas she was lost in her thoughts, with watery eyes, her smile absent. My mom was filled with love for us and a sinking sadness. When we were done, we got inside our old Crown Victoria, opened the windows, and buckled up to drive with no a/c under the Puerto Rican sun. It was like broiling our pain in an oven.

The energy company cut our house power. My brother and I played in the dark and pretended a hurricane had hit the island.

a prayer for the ones who lost all

Inhale:

Dios.

Exhale:

¿Por qué me abandonaste?

domestic romance

madre, how I want you madre
madre womb, madre blood
your breasts inside their caves
and the birds on the clouds
with adobo in her hands
she stands on her patio
white clothes, white flags
her bodies in the water
invisible how I want you invisible
under island sun, woman-grass
woman-flesh, woman-ashes

the women I grew up with

Mami of My Childhood

My dad was the roof over our heads, the food on the table, the name we needed to behave for, the clothes we wore. Mami of my childhood was the home we had. When I was a toddler, she and I were in a very bad car accident. She hit the wheel with her head and broke the front glass with her face while I was in my car seat in the back. I remember the doctors were worried about my bruised chest. The car-seat belt burned me, and my chest was blue. They kept asking me if it hurt, afraid that I had a broken clavicle.

I stared at my mom, at her bleeding face, and didn't say a word. Maybe if I stared at her long enough she wouldn't die and leave me alone. My chest was bruised because of my seatbelt, and my mom's face was almost unrecognizable because she was not wearing one. That was the way she loved us. It was always about everyone else and never about her.

The Women Who Share My Blood

My mom waiting for my dad. My abuela who cleaned and changed her children's diapers and the children of her children. The cousins, the aunts, all my women. They endured husbands who yelled or fisted walls when they were angry, who came home drunk after a night with their friends or with a mistress, so that I didn't have to. So that I could leave any man and any house at the first blow, the first lie, the first drunkenness, the first time they cheated. They all stayed to give me a house so that the house would give me food, education, a better life. So I would not have to stay with the boyfriend, with the husband, with the lover, or any asshole man like theirs. I wonder if I've betrayed them when I've stayed.

The Marthas or the Women Who Sacrificed for Me

Mami's back pains. Calluses on Abuela's knees from praying, from kneeling to clean bathtubs. Bunions. Nails stained with achiote. Water bags on their heels. Dark circles. Wrinkles. Soft-Scrub hands. Clorox. Fabuloso. Tilex. Cleaning and cleaning the houses that their men soiled with shit. Learn from me, nena. Study, nena. Don't depend on any man. Study. Study. Study. But sometimes I lose my books. And sometimes I mutate into them when they're not watching.

Sara

Sara found her husband dead inside the bathroom. He fell while taking a shower. A thirty-year-old man doesn't fall in the shower unless he is wasted. Unless maybe he wasn't showering and broke his neck when he fell from the toilet right after shooting drugs. Unless he died of an overdose before breaking his neck in the shower. Maybe he was dead already when he fell. I knew this. She knew this. People pretended not to know. Ever since it happened, I feared my husband would die when he went inside the restroom or left the house late at night.

How could she survive his death?

Maybe the same will happen to me.

Why her? Why not me? Why us both?

marriage addictions III

You brought home the street hunger. You turned on the stove, took out the milk, the bag of cornmeal while I made sure you didn't burn anything. That you didn't burn yourself. I was cleaning behind you, tripping over you with every step, every half turn like a failed attempt to dance a son Cubano. Without the party. Without the joy. Without the music. You were annoyed as if I were stepping on your feet. You never understood how difficult it was to clean dry cornmeal from a pot, from the ceiling, from the cabinets, from the table, from the floor, from the clothes, from a plate . . . you only knew how to spill it. From the stumbles and our fractured dance in the kitchen you went to the dining table spilling cornmeal on your way. Absent, with full veins and an empty stomach, you sat at the table and tried to eat a few bites without falling from your chair. I sat at the table with you and shook you on the shoulder to keep you awake, but I stood up and went back to the kitchen because I didn't want to see you anymore. You fell asleep with your face on the plate. I cleaned the mess on the floor while it was still fresh. I waited for you to wake up to take off your shirt and clean your face.

You took the keys I hid inside a kitchen drawer, opened the front door, and left our house. When I got out of the bathroom to get ready for bed, I realized you were gone. I went back inside the shower and stayed under the warm water as long as I could stand, until my fingers were wrinkled and my skin extra clean. It distracted me from the fear of a panic attack. It helped me to avoid thinking about all the bad news I could get.

What if he overdoses?

What if the police call me to identify his body?

I dismissed the thoughts.

He has experience shooting drugs. He won't make a mistake.

I was looking for you in Sabana Seca and saw from a distance a homeless man crossing the street. Except, it was you. I couldn't recognize you. I called your name, and when you turned, I saw your face. Your forehead injured, a river of blood running between your big, green eyes that didn't recognize me either.

"Where are you going?" I yelled from inside the car.

"I'm going home, don't you see?" you answered from across the street with your eyes lost, yourself lost. You were walking in the opposite direction of the way home, and I wondered for how long you'd been trying to return.

"Get inside, I'll take you home." You didn't look at me, but you got inside the car. Maybe you were trusting the voice that promised to take you home.

Can you take a picture of a soul breaking?

I came home from work and found you on the floor. I threw myself on top of your body and shook you as strong as I could to see if you were alive, as if I could bring back your soul from

the dead. You opened your eyes. I remember your blank stare.
Your white eyes. I remember things I don't want to remember.
That I don't want to write about. Consider them written in this
space:

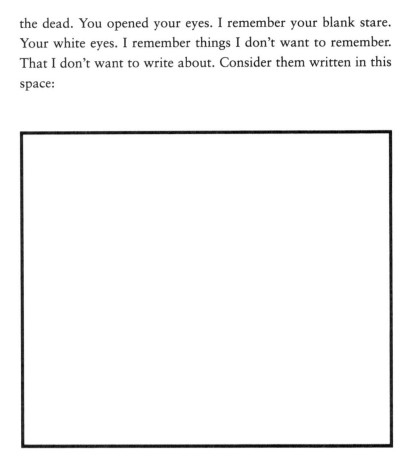

"I don't want to be married to you anymore," I blurted out
on a Sunday morning. You went to live with your parents. I
stayed by myself in a haunted house.

I received a call from a neighbor a few days after you moved
out. "I believe your house was broken into," she said on the
phone. I hurried home from work and saw the broken kitchen

window. Our TV on the ground outside. Your body coming out from the window. I pushed you as soon as you came out of the window.

"What's wrong with you? Are you insane?" I yelled, and you didn't respond.

You took the TV from the ground, and I took it from you.

"If you ever come to this house again, I'll call the police," I told you.

"Fuck you," you responded as you stumbled into the street.

A woman drove by, and you got inside of her car. She sped off. Until I no longer saw you.

a hopeless prayer

Dios todopoderoso ayúdanos a llegar sanos salvos y tranquilos.
Dios todopoderoso ayúdanos a llegar sanos salvos y tranquilos.
Dios todopoderoso ayúdanos a llegar sanos salvos y tranquilos.
Dios todopoderoso ayúdanos a llegar sanos salvos y tranquilos.
Dios todopoderoso ayúdanos a llegar sanos salvos y tranquilos.
Dios todopoderoso ayúdanos a llegar sanos salvos y tranquilos.
Dios todopoderoso ayúdanos a llegar sanos salvos y tranquilos.
Dios todopoderoso ayúdanos a llegar sanos salvos y tranquilos.
Dios todopoderoso ayúdanos a llegar sanos salvos y tranquilos.
Dios todopoderoso ayúdanos a llegar sanos salvos y tranquilos.
Dios todopoderoso ayúdanos a llegar sanos salvos y tranquilos.
Dios todopoderoso ayúdanos a llegar sanos salvos y tranquilos.
Dios todopoderoso ayúdanos a llegar sanos salvos y tranquilos.
Dios todopoderoso ayúdanos a llegar sanos salvos y tranquilos.
Dios todopoderoso ayúdanos a llegar sanos salvos y tranquilos.
Dios todopoderoso ayúdanos a llegar sanos salvos y tranquilos.
Dios todopoderoso ayúdanos a llegar sanos salvos y tranquilos.
Dios todopoderoso ayúdanos a llegar sanos salvos y tranquilos.
Sanos, salvos y tranquilos, sanos, salvos y tranquilos. Sanos,
salvos, sanos, salvos, sanos, salvos, sanos, salvos, sanos, salvos,
sanos, salvos, sanos, salvos, sanos, salvos, sanos, salvos, sanos,
tranquilos, tranquilos, tranquilos, tranquilos, tranquilos, tran-
quilos, tranquilos, tranquilos, tranquilos, tranquilos, tranquilos,
tranquilos, tranquilos, tranquilos, tranquilos, tranquilos, sanos.

madera mala

The glass crib
I built, lays
empty. You died,
unconceived.
The grenades
I nursed, exploded
on my chest
I'm still
looking for my arms.

the untamed women

Titi Elisa o La Mala Madre

Titi Elisa couldn't go out without asking for her husband's permission. Mami became a mediator, a Virgin Mary interceding to Jesus for the sinners. "It will be quick, let her come with us to get some ice cream," my mom would tell him. She disapproved of his behavior, but she wanted to spend more time with Titi Elisa. One day Titi Elisa walked out on her husband and her children. The family then called her mala madre.

Titi Mirna

Titi Mirna was the first one in my mom's family to go to college. Her ex-husband never sent a penny for them, but her three kids didn't die or starve. She made a new way for herself, an unwalked path that had never before been traveled by any woman in our family. But they didn't see that. They were too sad for her, always hoping and praying that a good man would come to her rescue.

Anabel

Anabel decided to "be like a man" and earned everyone's criticism. "Poor Anabel, so many college degrees, so educated and sin marido." Professional. Divorced. Multiple boyfriends. Focused on her own success and having different men for companionship without being domestic. Why did they pity her?

Concubina

Is what my grandma named my cousin's girlfriend when they decided to move in together. My cousin got to keep his name, Javier.

Happy Wife

Is the name of an ice cream flavor from Milk + Sugar in Houston. I ordered it to prove to my friend that happy wives were a myth and that a man named the ice cream. If I lost my bet, at least I would know what a happy wife tasted like. Sweet cream base and house-made almond pound cake. When I put it in my mouth it was creamy and cold and it tasted of snow, or air, or a ghost.

a prayer for acceptance

Inhale:

I tried.

Exhale:

Like the women of my life tried.

abuela mery before us

Her name faded in a corner. A smiling woman, tall, rooted between plátanos and panas. Before time wrinkled illusions. Strength. Where the green and the white were buried? The blue sky, her red lipstick. In which day the cheerful woman was lost, in which war? Her spark. Folded like a picture that doesn't fit inside a husband's pocket.

aislamientos
SHORE

uno

exiles

the dual or multiple

If I had to talk about who I am or how I've become or where do I come from, I would have to split the story in two, and probably stay in between as an observer, as an outsider to my own life. I've had two lives and now also two languages. Sometimes I forget in which one I exist.

I'm the one in-between sizes, in-between countries, in-between categories. Sometimes I don't know if I should shrink or expand.

prayers for the ones
who emigrate

Inhale:

No matter where I go.

Exhale:

I'll never feel home.

diasporic essay I

Mami drew her first words in other coordinates, and she made me a way in exile with her first steps. I had to change my path. I tried the normal life, and home escaped my hands. I buried my wedding dress in the closet. The rules died when the locks were broken and the doors were opened. A pair of wings was born through my ribs. I embraced the roads that she opened for me with her feet, carrying an empty womb and broken mirrors.

diasporic essay II

Mami the inattentive girl, her stare lost in another part. The distracted, the observer who feels less than others, she does not exist in the world like they do. Her time is different, her head draws spiraled universes. The distinct one, the one who doesn't do well in school, the foreigner. In the midst of displacement her life celebrated in birthdays. Home is built where candles are lit and feliz cumpleaños is sung. Far from the island. The birthday girl stands grounded and lost.

diasporic essay III

Abuela, you taught me to work hard, but working hard in the United States is never enough for a Latina. I wonder how things would be if my tongue were made loose and English possessed me with synonyms, verb conjugations, musicality, fluency. If English stripped Spanish from my DNA, my fatness, my big red hair. What would happen if English shrank me, shrank me, shrank me into a small, small, small, petite, tiny, skinny little white, blonde woman dressed in beige with diamond studs, a wedding band, and no gap between her teeth.

diasporic essay IV

Abuela, before I was, you were wings. You had passport stamps, residencies in other worlds. You gave birth to foreign children. Abuela, I was not the first one to leave the island, but I'm the only one that hasn't returned. I did not learn to sow, to cultivate the land, like you. Maybe that's why I did not grow roots. I undug my hands from the earth that touched yours, and my feet escaped behind them.

a prayer for the one who doesn't return

Inhale:

Help me to forgive myself.

Exhale:

For missing their lives.

Inhale:

When I'm far.

Exhale:

Keep them safe.

the women who are not the one

The One Who Dies and Resuscitates

I moved to Houston when I got divorced at twenty-nine and I was too fragmented to stay in the island. I moved there to spread my ashes in a land that was not a witness of my failure. In a place where I could feel dead without funerals, or sympathy. Where no one could bring me flowers. Away from my ex, before I was too tempted to fulfill my promise of staying with him till death do us part. I came to be a Jane Doe. And I was one, until I started coming back to life.

The One Who Exchanges Cages

I started undoing all the right things. Unwalking the good paths they forced on me. I did everything I wanted. I slept with as many men I could. Or wanted. Until I met a Palestinian guy. We shared that resilience of those who survive wars. Me: a survivor of a husband's addiction to heroin—and cocaine, and Xanax, and alcohol. Divorced from the man I loved for twelve years, suffering the loss of a church and most of my childhood friends, of a perfect couch, of a brand-new car, of family, of two dogs, of a goddaughter, of nice neighbors, of my in-laws, of hope, and of faith as I knew it.

He: a war refugee. Born and raised in Gaza, witness of real wars. The wars that movies are made after. Bombs, blood, destruction, tents, long lines for food. Exiled, and his family still living in Palestine. A visual artist.

We understood each other's darkness. I spent hours at his studio, surrounded by art, lying on his brown leather couch, watching him work while the music of *Mumford & Sons* or *Of Monsters and Men* played in the background. He made me feel less alone in Houston. A month into dating and seeing each other almost daily, I discovered he was married. Fuck. I did what I never thought I'd be capable of: I stayed for a little longer.

The Ones Who Are an Object

Who are we supposed to be but objects of desires, fulfillers of fantasies? A reflection of hungers. We put ourselves on red tables, sacrifices to the male gods. Naked, legs open, we become another. Mutate into drowned colors, shades of white, black, beige. Universes within us, hidden. Bodies taken. We are an it. Faces that want them. Wombs that receive their cum.

The One Who Gets Married and the One Who Gets Pregnant

Elena planned her wedding for months. A few weeks before the wedding she learned that her fiancé had gotten his ex-wife pregnant. That was the same year his firstborn turned eighteen and left for college. Elena was supposed to start a life with him without the ex-wife present in their minds. With the ex-wife pregnant with his second child there will be eighteen more years of alimonies and closeness. Elena married him anyway and helped him raise the child.

The ex-wife's firstborn was not enough to make him stay. Eighteen years later he got her pregnant again, and it still was not enough for him. He married Elena before she gave birth.

The One Who Was Victim of Brujería

I heard Abuela couldn't eat, she was disappearing from her body after finding out her husband had another woman. She was hospitalized without a diagnosis, suffered panic attacks. A strong woman made weak. "Me hicieron brujería," she said blaming her ailments on witchcraft. Instead of naming it grief.

The One Who Reads Feminist Theory

"There can be no love without justice," bell hooks writes. You wonder if the women in your life have experienced justice.

la isla

The motherland has never been a free country. How do you learn to be free if you've never seen freedom? How do you learn, as a woman born in an enslaved island, to be independent? To free yourself when your own country hasn't been able to. I left behind my mother. Daring to live a life better than hers. How does a colonized woman dare aim for freedom? I was born and raised to fear being left or abandoned. "Any day the USA could get tired of us and leave us to our own luck," they always told us.

We've never been sure of our relationships. *Estado Libre Asociado,* translated it doesn't have the same meaning, *Commonwealth of Puerto Rico.* The colonialism is disguised. Then you go through life and you don't mind relationships that have no definition. You are used to being owned without expecting anything in return. You are used to needing your owner, you need to be owned. You are afraid to stand on your own feet: independent.

If you are independent, you could be persecuted, end up in jail, you could get killed. Because if you want to be independent, you'll be part of a shamed minority. You have to become small because the smallest island from the Greater Antilles is Puerto Rico—"Look how small we are," our geography teachers always taught us when they pointed to the map. And there you are with the irreverence of trying to be big. You have to unlearn that you can't make it by yourself. They always told you, "The island can't make it by itself."

You are a woman, and you are an island.

dos

storms

the storms hit

I grew up loving hurricanes. In my Caribbean childhood, hurricanes meant days off from school, playing with friends under the rain, and hearing neighbors making jokes to each other. Hurricanes were the sound of their laughter. They meant people cooking sancocho and sharing Chocolate Cortés with crackers and queso de papa. It was calling everyone to make sure they were okay and had everything they needed. It was watching green palm trees dancing with the wind. It was lighting a few candles when power was out and playing Monopoly or singing to the sound of my dad's guitar and my mom's voice. Hurricanes meant quality time with family and friends. In our concrete houses, hurricanes couldn't harm us. We were home, and we were safe.

This hurricane is bigger than the island. It should hit Yabucoa around 6 a.m., and there are rumors people will lose their cell phone signals. My mom plans to change her voicemail message every day with an update on how they're doing. She heard in the news that they won't lose access to voicemail and people will be able to check their messages. I am not on the island, but I don't think that's possible. I keep calling her and waking her up throughout the night to check on them. I ask if they're scared, if they can hear the winds, if it's raining. The truth is I have nothing to say. It's the first time that the island awaits a category 5 hurricane, and I'm in Houston. I call for the third time at 3 a.m.

"The power is out," she tells me. "But it is not hot here because it started raining, so we're sleeping well," she says.

I stay quiet. She reassures me that they'll be okay, but another truth is that she doesn't know.

"Please, take care and don't go out. Stay away from the windows. I'll keep calling until there's no signal," I tell her instead of saying *Please, don't die* or *I'm afraid this could be our last conversation* or *I'm sorry for not being there* or *I'm sorry for moving away from the island.* We hang up, and I start scrolling for news in my phone. The hurricane gets closer. Noticentro promises to be on air with news coverage for the next 24 hours. I feel relieved. I lie on my couch with my laptop to stream the broadcast and check the hurricane on the radar. I feel like a small god watching over them.

[s]he who watches over you will not slumber . . .

I wake gasping for air. I am still on the couch, and it's 5:22 a.m. I see on my screen that the Noticentro livestream has gone black. I call my mom again. *Please, please answer. God please, please let me talk to them.* "Hi! This is the Ortega family. It's the first day of the hurricane. We're okay, and we're safe. God bless you!" I dial over and over again. Until my hope shrinks.

I try to find news on my phone, my laptop, through friends.

A short video on Facebook. A man in Toa Baja is on the porch of the second floor of his concrete house.

"This is like nothing we've ever seen before. This is the highest we can go in the house," he says.

He points with a flashlight to the street. Currents of muddy water are invading his house. The video image shakes. The wind nearly rips off his clothes. His daughter starts screaming before dawn.

My friends from la diáspora post social media statuses asking for prayers. In English. We're the only ones left to pray in Spanish. *Por favor, Dios, por favor, por favor, por favor, por favor . . .* We've lost our words.

I text my friend Ana in Boston:

> *Have you talked to your mom?*
> *I have no news from my family*

She answers:

> *last time I talked to her she was locked inside of the bathroom with her dogs she thought the wind would rip off the windows*
> *i can't talk now*
> *i just can't*

We're waiting for the sun.

It's noon in Houston. My body glued to the couch. My laptop resting on my lap. My right hand clicking the mouse frantically to refresh Noticentro's webpage. Nothing. I switch to Facebook. My screens own me.

A picture with an SUV and a car flipped over. The windshields smashed.

A high-rise lost its wall-to-wall windows and its balconies. Wooden houses ripped to pieces.

I keep dialing my mom's number.
And my dad's.
And my brother's.
And my aunt's.
And my grandma's.
And my uncle's.
And my grandpa's.
And my cousins'.
What if this time they answer?

It's 3 p.m. in Houston. Noticentro is still down. Laura Monzón, the meteorologist, livestreams on Facebook using her cell phone. A faint trail of mascara traces her jaw line. Her eyes are wide open as if she's witnessed a homicide. She talks to us, the Puerto Ricans in the diaspora. We need to be patient. Stay outside the island. There's no communication with any mayor. The state of the cities and towns is unknown.

They're fine. I tell myself. *They're fine.*

A text message from my mom's cousin in San Antonio:

Have you talked to your parents? Are they ok?
I worry about the rain and the flooding . . .
I don't answer. She adds:
At least they're all together in the house!
It never occurred to me that if I'd lost them, I'd lost them all.

La Plata dam overflowing. An image of the street that goes to my parent's house turned into a river. Currents of brown water drowning my parents' neighborhood.

It's evening. My friend Marina texts me from San Juan:
I was sweeping water out of my house for 8 hours
I'm ok.
It's been a practice of faith and patience
Weed helps

My grandmother's neighbor calls me from his landline. He went to check on her house and the windows fell off.

Abuela's white couch, stained brown
                    her spring flowers carpet drowned
        clown porcelain figures
                        beheaded on the floor
    broken bookshelf slats
            collections of memories lost
    a wood rocking chair where she'll never sit again
    cántame abuela *Ay Turulete y En un bosque de la china*

I feel an urgency to fix her house. I cannot stand by, keep waiting. I don't know what I'm doing outside of the island when everyone I love is there. I check the plane tickets. The next available flights are in a week and almost three thousand dollars. I am an island outside of an island.

It's 9 p.m. in Houston. I still have no news. I call and call and call. I have no luck. What if I fall asleep and they call me? What if I take a shower and I miss their call? I decide to change my voicemail message:

"Mami y Papi los amo. I'm okay. I miss you. I need to know you're okay. Almost no one in the island has reception. Please, leave me a voicemail and try to call me again. I'm going to keep calling you."

Ana texts me:
> *i talked to my friend eduardo*
> *if i don't hear about mom in the next two days*
> *he'll try to drive there*
> *he said there's no way to drive now*
> *and that there's no green left! i'm heartbroken*

A picture of a wooden house broken in half by a tree branch. A picture of a concrete house that slid through a cliff of mud. If hurricanes had color, Maria would be brown.

A CBS News reporter is on the island. He uploads a video to his fan page.

"Most cell phones have no signal and internet is down," he says. "The streets are blocked with branches and debris, but tomorrow morning our crew will try to go as far as possible to keep you informed." A promise for answers.

Ziad texts me:
>*How are you doing? How's your family?*

I cannot answer. He texts again:
>*Hey! Are you ok??? Do you want me to come over?*

I don't answer. I don't want to talk. I don't want to change my pjs, brush my hair, wash the pile of dishes in the sink.

Marina texts me again late at night:
>*Outside it looks as if a fire burnt the trees.*
>*There's no green left.*

I wonder if Maria stole the green or if everyone has become colorblind. *There's no green left,* they keep saying over and over. And I wonder if my father's colorblind eyes miss the green too.

It's 1 a.m. in Houston, and I can't sleep. I scroll and scroll and scroll for news. As if I can find my family in my phone.

I call my mom in the morning, and it goes straight to voice-mail: "Hi! This is the Ortega family. It's the first day of the hurricane. We're okay, and we're safe. God bless you!" It's day two.

I call in sick to work, again. I don't want to be far from my laptop, I don't want to talk to anyone until I hear from my family. A migraine, I tell my boss. He's Puerto Rican too. He must know I'm sick with fear.

I try to distract myself and survive the rest of the morning with the same song on repeat. I try to find the childhood faith that I have lost.

En tu dolor, Dios cuidará de ti
En tu dolor, Dios cuidará de ti
En tu dolor, Dios cuidará de ti
En tu dolor, Dios cuidará de ti
En tu dolor, Dios cuidará de ti

The wait and the thoughts are suffocating me. I need to get out of the apartment. I leave the mess behind and drive to the Menil Collection. I lay on the bench below my favorite tree. I open my eyes to see its branches and its foliage. As if I'm trying to see the green that my family can't see, as if I'm lending them my eyes from the distance. I repeat in my mind obsessive lines, invoking poetry as mantra, as prayer, *verde que te quiero verde, verde que te quiero verde, verde que te quiero verde,*
verde que te quiero verde
verde viento
verdes ramas
I blink and the tears come out.

I never thought that what started as love could end up in exile. Growing up, I never thought that one day I would live far from my family, my friends, the green mountains, the crystal-clear beaches. I never thought the island could be destroyed. The island was a promise of return.

It's noon. I scroll my phone trying to find missing pieces for my puzzle.

La diáspora starts organizing food drives. In New York, Miami, Orlando, Tampa, Houston, Dallas, San Antonio. An island outside of the island. We haven't heard from our families, but we'll do whatever we can to feed them.

"I am begging you, begging anyone that can hear us to save us from dying. If anyone out there is listening to us, we're dying," says the mayor of San Juan in a video.

I message Ziad:

> How the fuck you do this?!?!
> How can you deal with being here and
> your family in Gaza?

He answers:

> I try to call them as much as I can to hear their voices their
> laughter
> Call them! You'll realize that they are enduring things that
> they even make jokes about their situation that they're still
> connected to life and that they are strong. They might even
> try to
> calm you down

It's late afternoon. Back in my apartment, the images keep coming. Pictures from a helicopter. A message written with chalk, *S.O.S. We need water.* Wooden houses without roofs. Collapsed bridges. A dad trying to keep his son's head above water. An old lady crying in front of her house. Uprooted trees. Landslides. Upended graveyards. Floating bodies. Broken utility lines. Cell phone towers collapsed. Lost dogs. Naked mountains. An island drowned in mud.

It's early evening. My phone rings. Titi Carla's number is on the screen.

"Titi!" I answer, as if I am drowning and coming up for air.

"Patri, es Mami. We're . . . ," my mom's voice on the other side of the phone.

The call cuts out.

It's evening. My phone rings again.

"Mami?" I answer. "Mami, can you hear me???"

"Patri! I can hear you now, I can hear you now," she says. "We're okay. Don't worry. We might not be able to call you again because our phones have no reception. I had to walk a lot to find some signal, but please don't worry. We're okay. Everyone is okay. I love you. Are you okay?"

"Mami, I've been so worried about you. The photos on the news are so sad. I love you . . . I wish I was there," I say. I'm trying not to cry.

"Things are not like they say on the news, nena. We're fine. Things will be okay. Some trees fell, but nothing major. I need you to be okay," my mom answers.

"Mami, you have no idea."

I'm thinking she has no access to the images from rural areas, to the news that started coming. I become a reporter to let her know that the apocalypse came before its time. *Mami, you have no idea.* Or maybe she has an idea and lies to me when she says I shouldn't worry about them. They're together. I am the one who is alone and far from home.

"Don't watch any more news, please. Your brother is coming, and he wants to say hi. Hold on," she says.

"Patri," my brother's voice on the other side. "Everything is fucked up. I'm glad you're not here," he says. "We have no island."

broken house

she stole

the bed in which you never gave birth

your half-opened windows

your green couch
ripped off

the paint shade you couldn't decide upon
the walls

the zinc roof
she ran away with

the sweat
from your forehead
the calluses

on your hope
the ache

of your back
freshly cut

forevers   and always
coquíes

that sang in your backyard

orange flamboyanes
sunday naps

the plantains you couldn't harvest

                                  nor eat

memories

               that were left

   to be built

                     pending

        intermittent

       like the island itself

  your house

              could not

                       resist

   hurricane winds

             collapsed

next to a pile of wood planks

     ironing board

     microwave

     stove

     and the ground where we stand

ruta panorámica

The blue tarps
Never arrive
Or they arrive
Late
If they arrive

Blue tarps
That cannot dry
Tears
Nor ease the waiting

Do not arrive

Sometimes

Arrive

Too late

The blue tarps of FEMA
Never get here
In time
To dress
The void

And shelter us
From heaven
To hide us
From God
So we speak to God less

The tarps of FEMA
Arrive and do not arrive

After broken
Roofs
And empty
Houses
And the flight
Of families

The blue tarps of FEMA arrive
To invade
The greenery of our mountains
To announce
How many houses are left
Without roofs
To show us those
That still have theirs

So we can learn
To tally poverty

the one who sends boxes

I gather batteries for you like Mami gathered her orchids before the hurricane came. I gather batteries for you, as fast as I can, in the same way that a mother gathers her children to flee the war. I gather light for you. I gather the absence of darkness. I gather my pain. I gather myself. In boxes. For you. And I cannot talk to you, and I do not know what batteries you need. So I gather all the ones I can find AA, AAA, C, D . . . . And I wonder which ones your flashlight uses, and how many flashlights you have. I wonder if your radio works and if you can listen to the news. And if you have music. And if you have enough crosswords to replace your telenovelas. A grandmother should not be in the dark. And I wonder if you still have matches for your candles. And if the Sacred Heart of Jesus will have a candle for you. You, who has lit so many for him . . . . Your darkness calls me and I cannot see you.

How do I send you the sun in a parcel?

How do I send you light in a USPS Flat Rate Box? "What size do you need?" they ask me at the post office. "The biggest one," I answer. I walk with the boxes to my car, which is full of batteries of all brands and sizes. I open the trunk, which also has cans of Spam, fruit, soup . . . I wanted to send you food, but you asked me for light. You, the one who never asks and always gives. Light. I put all the batteries I can fit in the box, I put in three flashlights and I also put in my faith to illuminate you. I prepare two boxes instead of one, in case one of the two is lost, so that one of the two will arrive first. And before closing them I see that two cans of soup and two cans of fruit will fit. And I put them in. In case you get hungry.

the women who
survive hurricanes

In the island we build ourselves.

My house opens like the Superdome to shelter the victims of the hurricane. My house offers them showers with hot water. Plugs with electricity to dry their hair. A bed in which they can sleep off their grief and a toilet with water to flush away the hurricane. My house gives them a space to be in an emotional coma. To not have to say that they are fine. Nor that Puerto Rico rises. To make themselves invisible. To forget about the water that they had to push with brooms, the clothes they had to wash in buckets. My house is a refuge to shut down and close eyes. It gives them permission not to get up for days. It knows how to cure us from exiles and ends of the world.

In my house they can have a cell phone with signal, internet. They can watch news, be on social media, find out what happened to them. See the images and videos of what they were experiencing in the island. They are consumed by the guilt of having air conditioning, eating boiled eggs, drinking cold orange juices. For not being in the darkness, for living better than the ones they left behind.

In my house their anxiety to gather batteries, medicines, cans of food, electricity generators grows. So that their father can open his medical practice. So that light comes back to their houses in the island. In my house the images of the hurricane torture them. And they can't sleep trying to organize the supplies before going back to war.

The granddaughters who come to visit the abuelas who were forced into exile, stay at my house. They come to see them in case they don't return to the island. To say potential goodbyes. In case they die far from the island, before the island becomes safe for them again. "When can I go home?" the abuelas ask them. "Very soon," the granddaughters lie.

In my house we open bottles of wine to talk like we did before the hurricane landed, to forget that everything hurts.

My house in the diaspora becomes a shelter. There are vitamins, chicken soup, oranges on the kitchen counter. We are all sick. Between vomiting, diarrhea, and shortness of breath we somatize our orphanhood.

hurricane memorials

Where do we visit the dead,
the owners of the missing bodies?

> *Bury the unclaimed,* they said.

What if we have claims
but not a body?
Where do we lay them?

> They built a memorial
> in the shape of a hurricane.
>
> Buried the decomposed,
> the unidentified.
>
> Brought jazz,
> left plastic flowers
> under the heat

We piled up sneakers, sandals,
loafers, flip-flops, boots
of bodies stolen.

Tied their names
to our ribcages

until they faded.

.

tres
burials

boxes to carry

My therapist says I put everything in the same box.

The night you moved out of our house I went to a funeral. Luisito had been shot seven times. He was only nineteen years old.

Drugs. I blame it all on drugs. It was a tragedy that Luisito was lost to a bad path and died. People like him kill people like you, slowly. People like him sell cocaine, heroin, Xanax in exchange for money, control, belonging. People like you consume it to escape their lives, their bodies. Us, the families, pay the highest price, powerless, stuck in our lives and bodies. I was angry at Luisito for selling drugs to people like you and at you for buying them. I was sad that there was nothing I could do to save Luisito. To save you. To save our marriage.

How many bullets are needed to kill someone?

A week before Luisito died, you left our house late at night to shoot drugs. As time went by, I couldn't wait at home any longer. I had to leave the house and look for you. What if you were dying alone of an overdose, what if I could rescue you? The anticipation of your death haunted me. I could feel my heart punching my throat. My soul, shattered. I got inside the car to look for you and drove around Sabana Seca for what felt like hours until I saw you crossing the street. Blood was running into your mouth, your shirt. My husband. An open wound in your forehead. That was the night I found your body, wounded, wandering through the streets. But the man I married was not there, he was gone. There was a stranger inside his body, using my husband's body.

Abuela became a widow when I was eleven. I became a granddaughter without a grandfather. I slept every weekend next to her and she didn't stop crying until the crack of dawn. *Nena, no one knows . . . nena, no one can understand . . .* I filled in the blanks: [the pain].

Abuela never cried in front of others. Her pain, her deep brokenness was our secret.

I didn't want to become a widow. To cry myself to sleep, like Abuela did for a year. Her eyes became teary every time someone played boleros. I wondered if it made her think about Abuelo's vinyl collection of tríos or if it brought memories about him playing his favorite albums in their living room. The music was a reminder that he was not with us and she wouldn't dance with him again. I didn't want to get the deep dark circles that were born around her eyes the day Abuelo died.

Abuelo was very ill for three years, victim of an undiagnosed diabetes that damaged his kidneys and his heart. A rare case that never showed symptoms, until it was too late. He went through dialysis three times per week. Abuela dedicated her days to care for him as his health began to deteriorate. She fed him, dressed him up, sprayed him with perfume, took him to his treatments and appointments. She refused to let her husband go. Titi Carla found the best specialists. Papi wanted to donate one of his kidneys, but Abuelo's heart condition made it unlikely he could survive the surgery. They tried to keep him alive as much as they could. It's how I learned to not give up on the ones we love. Towards the end of his life, he was in and out of the ICU every month, only fourteen percent of his heart was working. One Tuesday my mom picked me up at school and told me my grandpa had died. I felt an empty universe growing inside of me, but I didn't cry.

I became obsessed with spirits, ghosts. I wondered if my grandpa could see me. Or if he would visit me at some point. How was life after death? Every night I had nightmares, and I felt the air thickening, like a fog.

You told me you fell on the sidewalk and hit your head. I felt my body getting cold as if my soul was detaching from it. I couldn't look at your face. I didn't want to see the wound, the blood running between your big, green eyes that stared at but didn't recognize me.

My dad was a small-town family doctor. The neighborhood

I grew up in had more kids than houses. Wounds happened on a weekly basis, and I joined him every time a neighbor called with a minor cut. Whenever a kid fell off his bike, broke an arm. I wanted to see the cuts, the blood, the stitching, the bones in the arm brought back together. I wanted to see my dad healing others. I wanted to learn how to close wounds.

On weekends, I watched a TV show called *The Operation*. In one episode they cut out a piece of a heart and it kept beating on the surgeon's hand after it was detached. I wanted to grow up and become a heart surgeon, to have pieces of hearts beating in my hands.

I was never afraid of blood. I was just afraid of yours.

My dad couldn't save his dad.

I couldn't save you.

"I won't make it to forty," you told me. I laughed to take the idea out of your head or perhaps mine because I believed you.

When I saw your blood, I knew our relationship had to end. I couldn't stay married to you and wait for death to take you. I felt a heavy, suffocating force so close to me, to our house, that

I could almost touch it. The invisible fog. I decided it was better to leave you than become your widow.

I remember the first time I saw you at a youth summer camp. I was fifteen and you were sharing from the podium how God saved you, how you no longer needed to experiment with drugs. You were seventeen. I believed you and God. I know you believed God, but addictions are not spiritual illnesses. There is a mind, there is a body. That's the part that church didn't understand and didn't teach us.

Once upon a time I was a child wanting you.

A child that believed in miracles and happy endings.

I was devastated by our separation, but I still went to my cousin's funeral. My aunt Gloria's only son. She couldn't stand or walk by herself. Her feet could barely hold her, as if her soul was lying inside the coffin next to Luisito. I couldn't stop thinking about how common divorces are and how damaging. A child growing up in the middle of his parents' war. Used by them as an anger mule, back and forth between two houses until he slowly stopped belonging. Their relationship was full of losses, and Luisito's life was the worst of them all. I thought it was for the best that we didn't have a child.

Luisito's funeral was five blocks from our house in Levittown. I feared death could be contagious, like a virus. Or a curse.

Titi Gloria became a childless mother.

Did God love us less?

My therapist insists I put everything in the same box. I see every loss connected to each other, interwoven, living in the same space. I process them together, like an ecosystem of grief.

Maybe I should get more boxes, create more labels:

> My grandpa's illness
> My grandpa's death
> My husband's drug addiction
> My husband's wounds, his blood
> Luisito's death
> Our divorce (is that a death or a wound?)
> Packing, leaving, losing the island (a death and a wound)
> and I don't dare to say more, I will run out of labels and boxes.

How can I stop associating losses with losses? Wound with wounds? Deaths with deaths?

After we separated your parents convinced you to go to rehab. I was glad you were doing better, and I resented you for not doing it earlier. For skipping the psychiatrist appointments I scheduled for you, for not sticking with the twelve-steps group. For not recovering while we were still together.

"I cannot forgive myself for everything I put you through," you told me the first time we met after rehab. "I'm too embarrassed to look at you." You didn't ask me for a chance once you were sober, but I didn't dare to offer it either.

Divorce doesn't always happen because there's no love left. Love doesn't always end with divorce. Sometimes we need other things. I chose to move from the island and put an ocean between us. If I'm honest, I waited for you the first year. Or so. I should thank you for not coming after me.

After the divorce there was a collection of catastrophes, big and tiny. Events that cut the remaining strings that attached us to each other. There were milestones that felt like minor deaths. The first social media photo of you hugging another woman. The first birthday that you didn't sing for me, the first Christmas that I didn't go to your parent's house, the first wedding anniversary after the divorce. The rites of passage in this loss.

Then there was the night you called to tell me you had a girlfriend. You wanted me to know before I found out through social media, so it didn't come as a surprise. *But I won't get mar-*

ried again, you'll be my only wife, you said at some point in the call as to reassure me that no one would take my place. As if it mattered, or as if that was what I wanted. I wanted for the story to be another story. The story of a husband who would never use drugs. A marriage that didn't end in divorce. A life, a home in the island. Children. Beaches. An impossible ending.

You posted the first picture of you two together. She tagged you in pictures of dishes you cooked for her, of road trips you took to beaches, caves, the rainforest. A few months after, you moved in with her, and she tagged you in pictures where you were painting the walls, mowing the lawn of your new house in Aguadilla. Our story was replaced with another one.

The pictures reminded me of the man I married at twenty-five. The man that women stared at when we walked down the streets of San Juan. The man that built a concrete wall in our backyard to keep us safe. The man you were before your failed dreams and your never-ending depression, before you lost your music school, before you started drinking, before you tried to heal yourself with the streets. Before the occasional fix turned into turbulent addiction.

Our love mutated into an old friendship.

You called one day to tell me that Valentina escaped through the front yard fence. There were rescuers trying to find her. Our dog. The dog we adopted after getting married—lost three years after our divorce. The next day you called to tell me she had been hit and killed by a car. You were sobbing, you were going to bury her in your backyard, you said I could join you, that we could have a ceremony for her. I imagined her pain and couldn't hold back my tears. The last thread, ripped. There was nothing left to hold us close.

After Valentina died, our phone conversations became less frequent. We grew further apart. You called on my birthday, and I called on Thanksgiving. I still liked to hear your voice on your favorite holiday.

I knew when you were not doing well, the trembling in your voice, the quiet sadness. I could hear when you were struggling with a relapse, and it reminded me why we were not married anymore. Take care of yourself, you know you have many people that love you. I always tried to find words to make you feel better. And I made sure to say goodbye in every call.

"Jay is missing. His family hasn't heard from him for three days," my brother told me on the phone on a Saturday morning. "It will be in the news today. I just wanted you to know."

"He's dead," I told him. "He's never gone missing like that before."

I was surprised at my conviction. I felt an empty galaxy forming between my chest and my stomach. Goosebumps all over my body. The fog numbing me. I lay on my couch and scrolled through my phone, looking for news. A Facebook post on Noticentro's fan page read, "Relatives of a man who has been missing since last Wednesday ask for citizens' help to find him. Jay Rivera Morales was last seen in Toa Baja on Wednesday, November 6. If you have seen him or have information, you can contact his family at the following numbers . . ." I couldn't stop looking at the picture. I took it on our anniversary right after you finished singing a song you wrote for me. You were holding your guitar, sitting across from me in our backyard, and I asked you to smile for the camera. Your big green eyes open, full of life.

I went through our last messages. You told me that you were writing songs again and that you were playing in a band. You asked me if I was happy, if I was still writing, if I liked my new city. Same old. You sent the last text: *Write your book!*

I loved you then almost like a brother or a child.

"Patri, Jay passed away," my brother called later in the day. "I'm sorry, you were right." I couldn't say anything. I just felt the universe expanding, trying to drown me. I think he said that a policeman found you unconscious on a street in Levittown the night you disappeared. You had an injury on your head, and you were taken to the trauma unit of Centro Médico, unidentified. You went through surgery. A nurse saw your picture on the news and called your family. By the time your dad made it to the hospital, you were dead, and he had to identify your body.

This is how our story ends. My first thought when I heard the news.

Another wound on your head, your body lying on a dead-end street, floating on a river of blood.

You died alone. Did you die afraid?

I couldn't stop thinking about the night I knew our marriage had to end, the wound, the blood on your face. I couldn't stop thinking about Luisito's funeral, my fear that death would find you. Valentina.

Who are you if the person you loved for twelve years passes away after you're divorced? Do you become an ex-widow, or do you stay an ex-wife?

Me lying on my couch, scrolling through the Sunday news. A video in Noticentro starts with you singing with your guitar. Followed by an interview with your dad, who was sweating, sobbing under a mask, saying how much he loved you. I read the banner on the video: *Jay died of a gunshot to the head.* The universe exploded in my chest.

One bullet ended your life.

Your voice in my head, *I won't make it to forty.*

You were not like Luisito. You were not supposed to die like him. Who would want to kill you? Who would leave you wounded on a street?

Four years earlier, I resigned from being a widow, and now there's a girlfriend to suffer your loss. I see her on her Facebook posts as I imagined myself. The way I thought I would lose you, the way I imagined my world ending when we wouldn't find your body for days, when we would have to name your cadaver. I grieved you before you were dead.

Now you were really gone. Two months before you turned forty, as if you were trying to fulfill the prophecy.

I asked Mami to throw away our wedding album. Now that you were dead, half of our album was dead. After the divorce, I kept the wedding album even though I never looked at it again. It was Mami's gift, and it was too beautiful to throw away, so I left it at her house, buried in a closet. I was scared about being in pictures with you now that you were dead. I didn't want the bad luck, the tragedy to reach me more than it had. There you were smiling, there I was joyful, there was the past of us. A life that existed only in memories and ashes.

Mami told me she looked through the photo album one last

time. "I cried when I threw it away," she told me. "Back then I loved him like a son." Marriages and divorces are never just about two people.

Last night I dreamed about your death. A flood, your body floating on dark water. A flood, you watching me watching you drown. My grief tried on you so many deaths. A car accident. Cancer. An overdose. I thought you would die of an overdose. I wanted you to live if staying alive was an option. My dreams didn't show me the stream of blood. The bullet. Your head.

Lightning doesn't strike twice in the same place except sometimes it does, multiple times.

I didn't go to your funeral. I wanted to remember you alive. Sometimes I imagine you didn't die, that we're estranged because we divorced and I moved out of the island. I imagine you healthy, happy, playing your guitar or building sandcastles on the beach with two kids and a new wife.

the women who are wrapped in sheets

Adriana

When I was eighteen, my father helped one of his best friends find his daughter, a medical student who had disappeared. Her parents hadn't heard from her after she arrived in Santo Domingo to start the semester. They'd been calling her for two days. She'd gone missing. Islands are the cradle of anguishes. Her father got on a plane to find her. A body appeared in a cane field, burned. *Is Adriana,* her father told mine on the phone. My father told him that maybe it wasn't her, that the body was burned, that maybe she was someone else's daughter. Her father replied, *how you wouldn't know who your daughter is even if she's burned?* And my father took a plane to join him. He arrived to the neighboring island with her dental x-rays confirming that her father had in fact been able to identify his dead daughter. Burnt. Raped by her taxi driver.

Keishla

A body wrapped in a bedsheet, tied to a block with wires, appears floating in the laguna San José. There is a missing woman, Keishla, the girlfriend of a married boxer. She is one month pregnant. We don't want the body to be hers, but we don't want it to be anyone's body. There must not be a woman's body drowned in a lagoon. We learn in the news that the body belongs to Keishla. Her boyfriend hit her on the jaw, left her unconscious, injected her with heroin that he bought at Llorens Torres, wrapped her in a sheet, tied her up with wire and cement blocks. He threw her into the lagoon so that she would drown with their baby inside her.

Hurricane María Antonia

Abuela, when you died, I was far from Mami, from the island. The hurricane Maria ended for us with your death. María Antonia, you started another hurricane. I traveled to bury you, to hold Mami motherless. My mother, an orphan. My mother, born to me a daughter. I helped Mami put your clothes, your leather sandals, your bags in bags. Without your body. She gifted me your long pearl necklace, grape shaped pearl earrings from your drawers, diamonds. Abuela, who will help me clean Mami's closet when she's gone? Who will be left to clean mine? Who will keep our pearls and diamonds?

camino a casa
OCEAN

after the three longest minutes

Stand in front of the restroom mirror and try to brush off the disappointment of another negative pregnancy test inside another trash can. It's not that you want children. You want a body that can make them in case you ever want them. Maybe you've learned not to. This time, blame it on a two-month pregnancy scare that mutated into openness and possible names. There's a new boyfriend outside, waiting for the result. Before the boyfriend, there was a husband. You should know by now that scares are unnecessary, as unnecessary as buying pregnancy tests. Think about the memes with ovaries, uterus, and periods as symbols of womanhood. Curse the women who post them. So many years worrying about condoms, pills, Plan B, when your body came with birth-control methods included. Think about coming out and telling him that if he stays with you, he might never be a dad. Or, that you can fuck and fuck and fuck and your uterus will stay empty. Feel that your body is defective, and that you are not a woman-woman.

abuela geo

Abuela, I might never be like you. I won't have a lifelong husband. Our blood might die with me. Abuela, did I fail you? Did I disappoint you? Abuela, forgive me because I didn't have a daughter, a redheaded granddaughter like yours, to rock her on a cane rocking chair, to sing *Ay turulete o En un bosque de la china* while I wait for her to fall asleep in my arms. Nor to tell her how I fell asleep in yours.

cooking lessons

Abuela taught my mother la brujería de la cocina. I wrote poems on the kitchen table. Calderos and spoons clashing, sofrito sizzling. The smell of recao dancing in the air. She shared the tricks of achiote, fried pork inside arroz con gandules, mofongo de yuca stuffing. *Un poquito de aceite, un chispito de sal, on a tiny bowl machaca un ajito,* stir the rice *y bájale la luz, pruébame esto* to see how it tastes. Maybe one day I'll regret not cutting onions, peeling yuccas, crushing garlic.

Mami showed resistance by not teaching me how to cook. My mother burned her hands so she could keep me away from the stove. The curse would end with her. The daughter who she gave birth to was not going to be a daughter made for a house. She was not going to spend her life sweeping, mopping, moping, folding clothes. The daughter she gave birth to would have college degrees. A career. Independence from men. She wouldn't have to look aside if her husband flirted with another woman.

When you don't know if you should end the relationship with the Iranian boyfriend, cook Fesenjoon. Dig your hands in pomegranates, nuts, onions. Let it simmer. You have to be patient. Stir it from time to time and make sure it does not burn. Wonder if it was the same thing your women did when they cooked fricasé de pollo and arroz blanco con habichuelas. Quiet. Absent. Lost in their thoughts.

after the hurricane

My mom calls me on a Friday to tell me that my brother quit his medical residency and she's afraid he could harm himself. *He told me he cannot get out of bed,* she tells me. *He destroyed his career.* My mom wants to take a plane to New York to bring him back with her to Puerto Rico. I tell her that she wouldn't know how to help him move out from his apartment, that she barely speaks English. I tell her that I'll take the first flight out of Houston, that I'll bring him back with me.

When does the hurricane end?

The week before, my brother was sitting in the waiting room of a therapist in New York and sent me a picture of the *New York Magazine* article "Maria's Bodies." In the picture, the old issue laid open on his lap, one of his hands pointing at the image of the shipping containers that were used to store the dead bodies. He added a text: "What are the odds?!? It seems I cannot escape it."

My brother was having nightmares with the dead. The ones he couldn't rescue on the medical brigades. The ones that died because there was not enough albuterol, no lisinopril, no insulin, no clean water to drink in the central part of the island after the hurricane. People died deaths that they shouldn't have, and my brother was there to witness it all. Without electricity, without hospitals, without equipment. Helpless. Now his mind was revisiting it all. He couldn't save them in his dreams either.

A year before my brother moved to New York to start his residency, he was still working on the recovery efforts when a reporter from the magazine reached out to him on Facebook. They wanted to learn about the hospitals, the deaths that were not reported. My brother agreed to help them on one condition: they couldn't mention his name anywhere. He didn't want to get in trouble when he applied for residency programs. *The hurricane in Puerto Rico has become a man-made disaster, with a death toll threatening to eclipse Katrina's. After the Storm: Puerto Rico's Morgues Are Overflowing. Six months' worth of rain fell in less than four days.* The magazine was at the office a year after to remind him his nightmares existed beyond his sleep.

I land in New York late at night. On the long drive to his apartment, I cannot stop thinking about the year before. How I was in Houston helping to find supplies and how my brother was in the island taking them to the poorest areas. I wonder now if it was worth it.

I step out of the Uber in Yonkers. The neighborhood is dark, you can smell the trash and hear the sirens of ambulances and police cars. Across the street, my brother waves at me. He looks like a zombie, and my chest shrinks.

I stay quiet inside of the apartment. He's staring at a wall, motionless. When he finally speaks, he says that he quit because the hospital was letting people die without helping them. The homeless people and the poorest patients had to wait long hours and sometimes it was too late. The doctors avoided them all, there was no one to claim the homeless, most of the patients didn't have insurance. *I cannot watch more people die because of politics. I cannot sit down and watch more people die from things they shouldn't die of.* I sit and listen. *I talked to every-one in charge, but they didn't listen to me. No one cares.* I was not in Puerto Rico watching people die from asthma. I was not in his residency when he found a young girl lying dead on a staircase.

On Saturday morning, I go out for a walk to see if it is easier to breathe outside the apartment. The city was worse than I imagined. I think that my brother didn't lie when he said most of the people in the neighborhood seem to be high or talking to themselves. There is more trash, more homelessness, more despair than I thought. It feels like I woke up in a post-apoca-lyptic city, in which everyone has lost everything and there is no hope or future left.

Back in the apartment my brother lays numb on his couch. The scrambled eggs I cooked for him lie inside the pan, untouched. I break the silence to tell him that we only have two days to pack his clothes, sell his stuff, and bring him to Houston with me. *I cannot leave so fast,* he tells me. I tell him that he can, that this is not the first time I had to pack an apartment in a rush. That I bought his ticket and it's nonrefundable. The truth is that now I know I cannot leave him by himself.

I take pictures of his mattress, couch, snow boots, and post them on Craigslist, write "owned for less than a year" on every post. I pack his clothes as he lays on his bed. *I'm not leaving on Monday,* he tells me, *I have things to do here.* I tell him that it's over, there's nothing else left for him in that city. Except to sell his stuff and leave. *I need to buy shoes for one of my patients before we leave,* he tells me and even though I don't understand him I agree to it.

On Sunday, I go with him to the only shoe store in the neighborhood. He buys a big pair of Nikes for his patient. *Her feet have ulcers because most of the shoes don't fit her,* my brother tells me. I walk with him to the homeless shelter, and we wait for her.

He seems relieved after he checks M.'s feet and gives her the shoes. On our way back to his apartment, I keep thinking about the tall old woman, the worn sneakers that she was wearing like slippers, her surprise of getting new shoes, her sadness when my brother told her he was moving back to Puerto Rico. *Who's going to take care of me if you leave?* she told him, and for the first time since I arrived, I saw tears in my brother's eyes.

He gave his roommate the couch we couldn't sell. He brought with him two suitcases full of clothes and a duffle bag with the set of pots and pans that Abuela sent him: two fry pans, two saucepans, one sauté pan, and a stock pot. On Monday morning, I fly to Houston with my brother through an orange sky.

Later that week, I visit Cy Twombly Gallery by myself. After the hurricane it became my hospital and my sanctuary. I sit in front of my favorite piece, *Untitled*. I wonder how do I name the unsayable? Three canvases bigger than me stand tall on the wall. Oil, acrylic, oil stick, crayon graphite. The scribbles, the fragmented words on the canvases were waiting for me, my eyes absorb the splashes of red, yellow, green, and blue paint. Seated on the wood bench, I can feel the air filling my lungs and my chest expands.

author's pic

I was born from your left hand. Abuela, I am your ink and your pen. I write. The light that sits on the table. The words that are. Truth. I speak. Sentences that you left unsaid. Stories that started in you and live with me. We fly holding hands to the spaces that were silenced. I take the voice that drowned in your throat and write you. The lives that were not and the ones that could've been. Ours.

the one who learns to swim in the ocean

The Puzzle

I was born a puzzle. To be dismantled and reassembled. I've been practicing my whole life. Learning where the pieces fit. And I stick myself together. Each time a little faster.

Mujeres de Barra

A woman alone in a bar, according to them, a whore. A man alone in a bar, a man. A cheesy women's magazine suggests that if you go alone to a bar you should bring a book with you. What the fuck? If I want to read a book, I go to the library. If I want to have a drink, I go to a bar. When a hostess sees me alone at the bar's entrance they ask if I want a table. I roll my internal eyes at them. I sit at the bar by myself, order vodka with club soda and lots of lemons or with tonic or a bottled beer, no glass. I watch sports on their TVs, talk to the bartenders if they are bored on their shift, or I enjoy being in silence. Men who read women alone in a bar as an invitation approach me and become puzzled when they realize I am a woman having a drink in a bar, like any man does. If I want to fuck, I don't need to go to a bar.

When I feel like smoking, I go to a Middle Eastern hookah bar and order a grape mint hookah with mint tea. The male servers offer to start it for me, and I decline their offer. I know how to suck hard.

When I miss the island, I go to a cigar house, order an Oliva Serie V or a Tatuaje with whichever aged Caribbean rum they have, neat. Small vanilla-flavored cigars, and the ice they expect me to order, are not for the woman I am. I enjoy smoking in the solitude of a space I am not welcomed to but nevertheless, I occupy.

The Matriarchs

I hug you abuelas, for all the worlds that you left behind. I hug myself for wanting to get where you couldn't, for being the women you were not. Hug me in permission to create worlds in which I do not have to disappear in front of a stove. For wanting to know beds that don't always give me a roof, for not breastfeeding children, nor sleeping grandchildren. Release me to walk the roads that I opened for myself with your backs.

Coral: Daughter of the Ocean

I silence the fears. Hear the water calling my name. Corals inhabit tropical oceans. Sexual and asexual. *Release gametes simultaneously, around a full moon. Corals can live on their own but are primarily associated with the communities they construct.* I jump into the blue water and swim away.

author's note

In this memoir, as in memory, I focus on some events of my life and not others. I changed names and identifying traits to protect others' identities. In some instances, I merged characters and adapted timelines and settings for narrative and clarity purposes, but I stayed true to the experiences as I remember them.

acknowledgments

Pieces and fragments of this work previously appeared, often in earlier versions, in *Fireside Fiction*, *Houston Public Media*, *Literal Magazine*, *Bridges*, *Crab Fat Magazine*, and *Grace and Gravity*.

Many thanks to my amazing editors Kristen Elias Rowley, Joy Castro, and Rachel Cochran for trusting my work and for making this book possible: it has been a dream to work with you. My deep gratitude and admiration to my professors and mentors Mayra Santos-Febres, Adrienne Perry, David Keplinger, Sandra Beasley, Dolen Perkins-Valdez, and Melissa Scholes Young: your generosity inspires me. My beloved Peppermints Emma Francois, Emily Holland, Laura Lannan, Cristi Donoso, and Austine Model: thank you for being my trusted readers and my writing community in DC, and thank you, Emma, for your support throughout every step of this book. Thank you, Susan Coll, for your friendship and for everything you've taught me: I am beyond grateful that we crossed paths. Many thanks to my peers and the wonderful faculty at the American University MFA program and to my Houston writing community, who welcomed me with open arms. Special thanks to Layla Al-Bedawi and Julia Rios for being my first readers when I started the adventure of writing in a borrowed language and for translating my words. To my former team and colleagues at Politics and Prose Bookstore, thank you for the work you do and for offering me a home in DC. My gratitude to every workshop facilitator and writer who provided feedback on earlier iterations of this work.

To my family and loved ones, living and late, thank you for your love and our shared stories. Papi, thank you for teaching me to love literature—this book is also for you.

works referenced

In order of appearance

Reference to Fher Olvera's "El dragón" (2010)

Reference to Federico García Lorca's "Romance sonámbulo" (1928)

"Qué . . . maravilla" *from* Alberto Cortez's "Qué Maravilla" (1975)

"Dios te salve . . . gracia" *from* Ave María prayer

"There can be no love without justice" *from* bell hooks's *Communion: The Female Search for Love* (New York: William Morrow Paperbacks, 2002)

Reference to Psalm 121 from the Book of Psalms

"En tu dolor, Dios cuidará de ti" *from* Civilla D. Martin's hymn "Dios cuidará de ti" (1905)

"Verde que te quiero . . . verdes ramas" *from* Federico García Lorca's "Romance sonámbulo" (1928)

"The hurricane in Puerto Rico . . . four days," *from* Mattathias Schwartz's "Maria's Bodies," *New York Magazine* (2017)

"Release gametes . . . full moon," *from* "Corals" by National Geographic

"Corals can live . . . communities they construct" *from* "Coral Reefs" by the National Oceanic and Atmospheric Administration

machete

Joy Castro and Rachel Cochran, Series Editors

This series showcases fresh stories, innovative forms, and books that break new aesthetic ground in nonfiction—memoir, personal and lyric essay, literary journalism, cultural meditations, short shorts, hybrid essays, graphic pieces, and more—from authors whose writing has historically been marginalized, ignored, and passed over. The series is explicitly interested in not only ethnic and racial diversity, but also gender and sexual diversity, neurodiversity, physical diversity, religious diversity, cultural diversity, and diversity in all of its manifestations. The machete enables path-clearing; it hacks new trails and carves out new directions. The Machete series celebrates and shepherds unique new voices into publication, providing a platform for writers whose work intervenes in dangerous ways.